Truckin' Up!

Donna Carver

PublishAmerica
Baltimore

First printing

ISBN: 1-59286-674-3
PUBLISHED BY PUBLISHAMERICA BOOK
PUBLISHERS
www.publishamerica.com
Baltimore

Printed in the United States of America

For that truck drivin' man of mine.

Contents

Chapter One
Alligator on the Zipper

We were riding north on Interstate 95 in North Carolina. The sound of the big diesel engine vibrated through my head as I watched the white dashed lines slip by on the dark road ahead. I had been riding as a passenger in this semi truck for only a few days at that time and it was an exciting new adventure for me. It was so different from what I had imagined. Riding high above the road, I looked down into the cars that we passed. It gave me a whole new perspective on everything. I saw people doing all kinds of crazy things while they were driving. People reading newspapers or writing notes, and talking on cell phones, women putting on makeup, businessmen juggling coffee and biscuits. There were people changing clothes or flossing their teeth (steering with their knees) and even having sex while driving in heavy traffic!

"Break one nine!" The voice on the CB radio broke into the cab of the truck.

Don grabbed the microphone that dangled from a bungy cord attached overhead. "Come on break!" he said.

"Northbound," the driver came back, "you got an alligator on the zipper at the 129 yard stick."

Don grabbed the mike again and said, "Preeshaydit

southbound. You're looking good back to the line."

Now, I was raised in Florida and it wasn't too uncommon to hear about alligators roaming around in neighborhoods or on highways but this was North Carolina in the middle of winter! "Did he say there was an alligator on a zipper up here?" I asked, somewhat confused.

Don looked over at me and grinned. "It's not a real alligator, it's the rubber off of a recapped tire laying on the zipper, which is the white striped line in the middle of the road."

"Why do they call it an alligator?" I asked.

"Well, if that thing gets caught up under your car or truck, it will chew up everything it hits," he said.

"Well, where is this alligator?" I asked.

"It's at the 129 mile marker," he said as he pointed to a small road sign on the side of the road. This one read 120. "You see," he started, "most highways have mile markers or 'yard sticks' that measure the distance from beginning to end of the road in each state. They start at 1 at the south and east ends and run higher as you drive north or west." We were headed north which meant that the "alligator" was nine miles north of us.

I watched the mile markers as we pass until I saw 129. Just ahead, straddling the striped line in the middle of the road lay a large jagged piece of rubber. One end of it curled up in the air, looking very much like an alligator poised to strike. A few minutes later, we saw a big truck pulled over to the shoulder with his emergency flashers on. Don took the mike and asked: "You OK over on the side driver?"

A voice came back: "Yes sir, I just hit that gator back there and it took out my break line. I got help on the way."

"10-4," Don said as he let the mike go.

"Those alligators are dangerous!" I said.

8

"They cause hundreds of accidents and hundreds of thousands of dollars in vehicle damage every year," Don said as he shifted to another gear.

"Why don't they outlaw them?" I asked. "Lots of large companies use recapped tires to save money. They have lobbyists in Washington who make sure that recaps aren't banned." Then he added, "It's a money thing."

As I listened in to the conversations on the CB radio, I soon realized that I didn't understand half of what was being said. I learned that since the 60's, truckers have used Citizens Band or CB radios for communications and over the years, they have developed a colorful language all their own. Truck drivers generally monitor channel 19 on the CB or "Sesame Street" as it is sometimes called because of the childlike behavior that is sometimes heard on that channel.

I was glad to have Don as an interpreter. He literally grew up in the trucking business starting behind the wheel on his daddy's knee and driving by the time he was thirteen. Yes, he is a driving machine. The man even drives in his sleep. Every now and then in the middle of the night while we are sleeping, he will reach around and grab one of my breasts and start shifting gears. Those first three or four gears are bad enough but when he shifts into high gear I have to put on the breaks.

Don had been driving trucks for more than twenty years when I met him and was well versed in "Truckers Slang." There is trucking slang to describe almost everything and I have listed a collection of over 400 truckers slang words and phrases in the chapter titled: "Truckers Slang." I have also listed "Trucker Cities" and the National 10 codes. The list of trucker's slang is by no means complete because new words and phrases are being born every day but I hope you will refer to it and enjoy it as you read this book.

Most drivers have a "handle" or CB name. Generally, a driver will use a handle rather than his real name in order to protect his privacy and anonymity. Most handles are cute names that distinguish each driver's radio personality. Handles like "Leadfoot," "Fast Lane," or "Speed Buggy" might describe a fast driver or maybe a driver that just wants to sound like he's fast. I've heard many handles such as "Spanky," "Corn Cob," "Skid Mark," "Side Pocket," "Wild Man," "Corn Flake" and "Mattress Monkey." Female drivers also have some cute handles like "Big Momma'," "Wild Flower," "Little Momma," "Queen Bee," "Soggybottom Sal," "Precious" and "Shake-n-Bake." My handle is "Sweet Pee" and Dons' handle is "Bloomer Snatcher," which might tell you a little bit about him.

A typical CB conversation might sound like this:

Driver 1: "How bout ya' Rain Man? This is Desperado. You got your ears on?"

Driver 2: "This is Rain Man. What's your 20? Come back."

Driver 1: "I'm headin' northbound at the 35. Where you at Desperado?"

Divers 2: "I'm on your front door about two miles. Where're you headin?"

Driver 1: "I got two drops in the Motor City. Then I'll have to call my travel agent to see where I'm goin' after that."

Driver 2: "10-4, I'm headin' for the home 20 for a few days and spend some time with the other half, roger?"

Driver 1: "I hear that. I haven't been home for about three weeks now and the warden is getting pissed. Roger?"

Driver 2: "I copy that."

Driver 3: "Break one nine."

Driver 1: "Come on break."

Driver 3: "You got a major cluster fuck on your side at the

73 yard stick. Both lanes are blocked up for about five miles."

Driver 2: "What happened up there, driver?"

Driver 3: "A roger ramjet hit a pregnant roller skate and caused a thermos bottle full of go juice to go greasy side up and spilled motion lotion on the blacktop. They got a meat wagon up there making a pick up and a dragon wagon pulling off the wreckage. The haz-mat crew is mopping up the mess but it's going to be a long while before they get it cleaned up so you might want to detour. 10-4?"

Driver 1: "I hear that driver. Well, thanks for the heads up. You're lookin' good back that way. The chicken coops are open and checkin' the tension on your suspension. 10-4?"

Driver 3: "I copy that, driver. Don't tense around that break check."

Now, just in case you didn't follow all of that, I'll explain. The first driver, Desperado, asks Rain Man if he has his radio on. Then the second driver, Rain Man, asks Desperado where he is located. Desperado tells him that he is front of him about two miles and asks Rain Man where he's going. Rain Man tells Desperado that he has two deliveries in Detroit and that he will have to call his dispatcher for his next destination. Desperado is on his way home for a few days to spend some time with his wife. While Rain Man is talking about his wife being angry about his long absence from home, a third driver brakes in to give them a warning about a bad traffic accident involving multiple vehicles ahead of them. The accident was caused by a speeding car, which hit a Volkswagon and caused a tanker full of fuel to turn over and spill diesel fuel on the highway. The ambulance is on the scene and a tow truck is picking up the wrecked cars. Firefighters are cleaning up the fuel spill but it will take some time to clear the road and the driver suggests that they might want to find a way around the accident. Desperado thanks the driver for the warning and tells him that there are no police ahead of him and that the scale house is open and weighing trucks. The driver acknowledges the road report and tells him to take it easy around the accident ahead.

"Break one nine for a radio check!" This is probably the single most used phrase on the CB radio. There are literally thousands of CB radios in use by truck drivers alone and they check on their equipment regularly. "Break one nine for a radio check!" … "Yeah, come on" … " I just got this radio and had it tweeked out. How's it sound?" … "You're treetop tall and wall to wall, driver. Just like my girl friend, she's puttin' out all over town!" A "Mud Duck" is a radio that sounds weak or garbled.

CB radios come quipped with FCC regulated frequencies and basic microphones. But, drivers often have technicians work on their radios to enhance sending and receiving capabilities. There are plenty of radio accessories available to dress out radios such as: high power microphones and antennas, audio features like echo, reverb, prerecorded responses and much more. Generally, an average radio signal can be heard for three to five miles in either direction. If the traffic is heavy and several drivers are talking in the area, they can "Walk on" each other causing distortion of signals between trucks. If a driver has his radio "Tweeked out" with power boosters and high-powered antennas, the driver can "Walk on" or interrupt transmission for other radios for miles around.

Some things you hear on the radio aren't very nice. For instance, when occasional fights break out over the radio. One driver may have pissed off another by driving too fast or too slow. He may have cut the other driver off in traffic or it might just be that a driver has had a bad day and just likes to start trouble on the radio. Bantering back and forth, they call each other all sorts of derogatory names like: "Harvey Wallbanger" (reckless driver), "Juvenile Delinquent" (someone pretending to be a truck driver), or a "Good Buddy" (a homosexual), as well as the usual four letter words one might hear in a heated argument.

"How bout ya', covered wagon. Why don't you get that dragon fly (drags uphill and flies downhill) out of the hammer lane and quit blockin' traffic?"

"Back down, windjammer (fast moving truck), I got a fat load (heavy load)."

"Well, quit knuckle draggin' (going slow) and put your foot in the gas hole and do it to it, good buddy."

"OK, bumper sticker (driver following too close), how about you eyeball me (meet) at this pickle park (rest area) up here?" In this instance, the language isn't too bad but in some cases, it gets pretty nasty and is hard to listen to. Personally, I prefer to use "cussin' cusins'" or words that sound like swear words. When the language get real bad on the radio, you just have to tune them out or turn the radio off until you get out of range.

Most drivers use clean language on the CB. Only small minority of drivers use fowl language and they may give the impression that all truck drivers are rough ridin' tough cowboy types. But for the most part, these men and women are average hard working people doing a hard job and often under difficult conditions.

Often, drivers will listen to the CB to help them stay awake. If you've ever been on a long road trip, you know how tiring it can be. So, imagine driving for eight to ten hours with few breaks before climbing into the bunk for a few hours of sleep. Then, after you jump right back into the drivers' seat and run straight into a traffic jam. If by some miracle, you arrive at your destination at the appointed time, you find out that you must still wait in line to be unloaded even though you have an appointment. Then you must unload forty or fifty thousand pounds of freight or pay a "lumper" or dock-worker to unload the freight for you. After it has taken the lumpers three hours to do twenty minutes worth of work you can collect your paperwork and jump back into the drivers' seat. Now it's time to call your dispatcher sends you two or three hundred miles to pick up another load that has to be a thousand miles away by the next morning. Try repeating that sort of routine day after day and tell me truck drivers got it easy. It's no wonder that they get a little "testy" sometimes.

After long hours on the highway, drivers can get a little bored and some will pick up the microphone to try and engage another driver in a conversation. Generally, the conversations are fairly dry but some drivers will take the opportunity to vent their frustrations about their jobs, the road, wives or girl friends and just about anything else. Some drivers will even try to pick a fight with another drivers just to pass the time.

There is still another breed of CB'er who doesn't have anything to say on the radio but feels the need to broadcast "something" for his fellow drivers on the road. I call them "Truckin' DJ's" because they key their mikes up in front of their stereo speakers. It makes most drivers mad because the DJ's usually plays music the other drivers don't like and as long as the DJ keeps playing his tune, no one else in the area can use their radios because of the interference.

"Southbound, you got a female pedestrian on the shoulder up here and I think she's lookin' for a ride." Hitch-hikers can a problem at times because you can never be sure what kind of person might be climbing into your truck. A lot of drivers make it a policy to never pick them up but occasionally they do. One day, Don picked up a young couple who seemed to be down on their luck. He said that when they got into the truck he noticed a bad smell and that within minutes he had to pull the truck over and make them get out. There was a woman down in Florida a few years back who would try to get rides with truck drivers, eventually killing and robing them. She was eventually caught but, there could be others like her.

Chapter Two
The Road

I have seen and heard many crazy, horrible, and wonderful things on the road. Each day brings something new as you watch the sun rise and set in a different place. My sense of time and place became distorted as we rolled past the rugged mountains and through the valleys then onto the plains of this country. I couldn't help but be in awe of its great beauty. The only thing that seems to spoil it all is what man has put here. It broke my heart to see all the trash alongside of the highway. Most truck drivers are pretty good about not littering and some states are better than others about keeping things picked up but everyone should do their part.

Most of the time, drivers spend seemingly endless hours driving down the road with little more than the drone of the engine ringing in their ears while the world passes in front of the windshield. But, they never know when they might see or hear something that will make them laugh, cry, or just plain mad. The beautiful scenery that gently drifts past the window can quickly change into concrete and steel with the rush and hurry of the people who live there. A seemingly easy ride around a bypass or a beltway can turn into a multiple car pileup where people are hurt or even killed. A ride that should have taken thirty minutes may delay the driver for hours costing precious time and money.

One of the first and worst accidents I have seen on the road was down in Florida. It started raining suddenly and we watched as a small four-wheeler a few cars in front of us slammed on breaks. The car went out of control and slid across the median "comedian strip" and into oncoming traffic. A man in a green Caravan hit the little car and the man was ejected from his vehicle and onto the road. The Caravan came down on top of the man, cutting him in half. Meanwhile the car that had crossed the comedian strip hit yet another passenger car. We heard later on the CB that a young woman and her three children were killed.

One spring day as we rode south through the mountains of Tennessee, we heard a warning on the CB that there had been a terrible accident on the road ahead and that the southbound lanes were blocked for ten miles. We looked at the road atlas, a must for any driver, and found an alternate route on an old highway that paralleled the interstate and would bring us out past the accident. We exited the interstate and began driving on a narrow winding road full of hairpin turns that wound around the side of the mountain. On the driver's side of the truck, the side of the road dropped off sharply. We looked down and saw a beautiful white-water river winding along the side of the road. The water swirled and foamed as it washed over the rocks and boulders. A man in high waders stood on one of the larger rocks holding a fly-fishing rod. He gracefully sent his fly back and forth over the water. It was like seeing a Norman Rockwell painting in motion.

Driving conditions can add still another factor to the driving experience. I had seen Don drive through all kinds of weather. A clear calm day is ideal but that doesn't happen every day. As we drove through a violent storm with blowing winds, I realized that the trailer we were pulling was acting like a large sail and we were being blown hard. Don struggled with the steering wheel at times trying to keep the truck on the road. While many four wheelers were pulling off to the side of the road to wait out the storm, we had to go on to make our appointment.

White and glistening thick on the ground, the snow was like a creamy white icing on everything. It was wonderful to see, especially for a Florida girl who hadn't seen much of it. But as we continued north the skies grew gray and it began to snow heavily, almost completely obscuring our view of the road. Don said he hoped that we didn't have a "whiteout": when it gets so bad that the road completely disappears. We saw where many cars and trucks had slid off of the road and into guardrails and ditches.

When we got off of the interstate, the roads hadn't been salted and plowed as much as the main highways and it became more and more difficult to drive. Even driving at very low speeds we were very nervous. As we approached an intersection, we saw the light was changing and Don prepared to stop the truck. He slowed the truck and as he checked his rear view mirror he said, "My trailer is sliding around." I looked and could see the back of the trailer sliding forward on the icy road. It looked like it might come around to meet the front of the truck. I could feel the cheeks of my backside grabbing the seat a little harder as Don pulled the trailer back into to place and brought the truck to a safe stop. I was thankful that there was so little traffic in the area but then again maybe only crazy truck drivers try to drive around in conditions like that.

We were in Texas last spring, sitting in a truck stop café. I could overhear the driver in the booth behind me talking to his wife on the phone. "Yeah baby, I know it's been six weeks but I gotta' go where they send me. I'll try to get my travel agent to send me your way but you know I can't make any promises." I could hear the frustration in his voice as he talked. "OK, put Jimmy on the phone. Son, You're the man of the house till I get back so, you help your mother take care of things OK? Yes, I know your mother says that she's in charge but she still needs your help. No, son, I'm sorry. I won't be there for your birthday next week but maybe I can be home for the Forth of July."

It was the middle of May!

I felt bad for that driver and his family and as I looked around at the other drivers in the truck stop, I wondered how many drivers, both men and women, had to be away from their homes and families, missing all those important birthdays and holidays. They literally watch their children grow up in photographs. "The infidelity and divorce rates must be pretty high for truck drivers." I said after the man left. Don looked at me and nodded. He had already been through it with a previous marriage and children. He knew exactly what I was talking about. He told me that there is a wide variety of trucking jobs out there. In some of them, the driver will get to go home every night and in others he may be away from home anywhere from two or three days to two or three months and for some much longer. There are even drivers who *live* in their trucks driving year round.

Now that I've been married to a truck driver for a while, I've experienced what most truckers' wives go through. We hadn't been married long when Don had to go out and leave me with the house and kids. Watching him drive out of the driveway, I realized that there was a chance he might not come back. My heart sank like a lead weight. Truckers die on the road every day and I waited each night for his phone call telling me everything was all right. Meanwhile, I had to take care of the household and deal with the kids' problems alone. I spent many long anxious nights wondering how I was going to deal with his absence. Once the kids were grown and moved out, I decided to go with him.

I really had no idea what I was getting myself into as I climbed up into that truck. I am an average woman, well educated with a fairly normal upbringing. I had raised children, worked and taken care of the house for more than twenty years. None of that prepared me for the adventure I was facing. I hadn't traveled much and I was excited that I was going to get to see some of the country. Although it's not the typical first class tour, I can honestly say that I have seen a side of this country I never knew existed and challenges that I never expected.

There were several construction "destruction" zones along the entire stretch of highway on I40 in Arkansas and it made for a very rough ride. As soon as we hit that road, the truck started bouncing up and down. I was already suffering from PMS and my breasts were sore. With every bounce, the pain shot through my breasts and I held my arms across my chest to keep my breasts from flopping around.

At the time, I was wearing an under wire bra. After driving 280 miles across Arkansas on that washboard "boardwalk," I was tired, my breasts were very sore and the wire in my bra had worked it's way out of the bra on each side poking me in my ribs. So much for that new under wire bra! I cringed a few days later when I found out that we would have to drive right back across Arkansas. I decided that I should have a good supporting bra. I ended up getting a sturdy sports bra. It holds my breasts in tight. The next trip across Arkansas was a lot better. No more flopping around for my girls!

Another problem I had was the lack of a bathroom in the truck. Bathroom breaks are few and far between, especially when you're fighting a deadline, "on a mission." I solved part of the problem by putting a large plastic jug in the truck to pee in. One with a handle and wide-mouth opening is easiest to use. Although it's difficult to use on a rough road and it has to be emptied and cleaned from time to time, it sure beats trying to hold it till we get to a bathroom.

We were driving in bumper to bumper traffic around the Washington beltway during rush hour traffic on a Friday afternoon. We were doing about ten miles an hour and at times we came to a complete stop. We were fighting a deadline and like most of the drivers in that break check, we were getting pretty frustrated. "Break one nine!" A voice came in on the CB.

"Come on break," Don answered.

"What the #@&*# is the problem up there northbound?" the driver asked.

Another driver answered, "Well, there's a guy in the middle of the road up here trying to shove butter up a bobcats ass with a knitting needle and he's having a hell of a time." The vision in my head was too much. I had to laugh.

Along almost every major highway are small white signs that read: Slower Traffic Keep Right. It seems that a large percentage of car and truck drivers completely ignore this sign. At times this can present a real problem not only for truck drivers but for car drivers as well. A car or truck in the second lane traveling slower than the traffic around it forces drivers behind him to pass on the right. If there are vehicles in the right lane who are also traveling at a slower rate of speed it can cause a backup in the flow of traffic. This creates a "rolling road block." An opportunity for accidents is created as cars and trucks begin weaving between the lanes trying to get around the slower vehicles. A good way to know if you are traveling in the right lane of traffic is to see if drivers are passing you on your right side. If this happens, you should move into the left lane of traffic and drive the speed limit. Let the other guy get the ticket.

Don has had his share of breakdowns on the road and has encountered many unscrupulous mechanics who try to take advantage of drivers and trucking companies by gouging the price of their services. One after noon near Clines Corner, New Mexico, a tire blew out on the back of the truck. Don slowed the truck down and pulled off of the road. Moments later, the driver of a TBS Tire Service truck, who had been parked at the off ramp like a vulture waiting for his next victim, pulled up behind the truck.

After careful inspection of the damaged tire, the service man quoted Don a price of $570.00 to change the tire and replace it with a recapped tire. Shocked by the price, Don asked the man if there was another shop somewhere down the road. The man told him that the next shop was 75 miles away. Refusing to pay such an exorbitant price, Don decided to try and make it to the next shop. He only drove twelve miles before finding Lisa' Truck Center in Moriarty, New Mexico. They only charged him $187.00.

I got my first taste of road rage when we were driving southbound on Interstate 95. We were about a mile from our exit, which had two lanes. A mobile home mover, "mobile modular residential commercial transportation relocation technical specialist" and two escorts were in the lane on our right and were going to take the same exit that we were. We had passed the mobile home and were riding next to the front escort, which was being driven by a woman. Don got on the CB and asked her if she would move over to the far right lane so that we could get off at the exit. She ignored his request and continued to drive in the second lane.

We were unable to pass the escort in time to make the exit so Don got on the CB and asked the escort driver again to please move over one lane. She looked up at us and continued to ride that second lane. Finally, with only seconds to the exit ramp, Don picked up the mike and told the escort driver that he had to get off at this exit and that he was coming over to that lane. He eased the truck over toward the second lane, forcing the escort driver into the granny lane. She picked up her mike and started cussing at us, saying that we had tried to run her off the road.

It infuriated me that she had ignored our requests for her to move over and allow us to use one of the two lanes on the exit ramp so I picked up the mike and said, "We tried to ask you to move over and you ignored us. You're suppose to be a courteous driver and share the road." She came back and said, "You guys need to learn how to drive on the highway." I said, "Just because you have a yellow flashing light on your car doesn't mean you own the whole road!" She began calling me some pretty bad names and I returned with much the same for her. I was getting really mad by now. I picked up the mike and told her to pull over and I'd be glad to kick her butt. She continued on driving and cussing. I tried several times to get her to pull over but she wouldn't do it. Finally, she and the mobile home she was escorting exited off the road.

I continued to fume over the incident for several miles until I realized that I was experiencing road rage. I giggled at myself that I had gotten so upset so quickly but now I realized why so many drivers get road rage. A lot of cars and truck drivers don't consider the other drivers on the road around them. They drive as though they are the only ones on the road and sometimes cause the drivers around them to resort to whatever means necessary to get where they are going.

One summer evening, riding north on highway 4 in Florida, he heard a driver holler over the CB, "Dammit boy, would you look at that!"

"What is it driver?" another voice asked.

The first driver said, "There's a couple in the four wheeler up here. She' got her head in his lap and she ain't sleepin'!"

"Where are they at, driver?" I didn't realize that I was such a voyeur until I started looking down into cars from the seat of the truck. We could see the four-wheeler that the driver was talking about. It was a Mustang convertible and the driver appeared to purposely driving next to the truck drivers' window so that the drivers would be sure to see what the woman was doing. As we drew closer to the car, I could see the driver stretched out in his seat with one hand on the wheel and the other lying across the woman's back. Her head was bobbing up and down in his lap and there was no doubt as to what was going on. The man drove is car next to Don's window for several minutes before slowing down to catch the next truck. "Dammit Driver!"

We were driving northbound around Atlanta, Ga. when the terrorists attacked the twin towers in New York. The traffic was heavy, as usual, and we heard the usual CB talk on the radio when suddenly a driver broke in and said that a plane had flown into a building in New York. I got up, walked back to the sleeper and turned on the TV to see if there was anything about the incident on the news and like so many others, I watched in horror as the second plane hit. Within a couple of hours, the highway started to empty of traffic. Trucks and four wheelers alike were pulling off of the road to listen to their radios, watch the news on TV and call to check of friends and family. Some people got out of their vehicles and stood in shock and amazement while others just cried.

Two weeks later, we had a trip to New York and as we passed Manhattan, I could see the awful gray smoke still rising from the large crater where the towers once stood. My heart sank and I felt a deep agonizing ache for all the families who had lost loved ones. American flags had been hung over the road from overpasses, telephone polls, and in front of houses everywhere we looked. The CB was full of talk about terrorists and many drivers were watching for possible terrorists in every car and truck they passed. We could literally feel the wave of patriotism and paranoia spread across the country during the next few weeks.

We heard a rumor on the CB that after hearing the news about the attack, an Afghani driver in a California truck stop, got out of his truck and started dancing around and shouting in victory. It was said that several weeks later, his truck was still in that parking lot but that the driver was nowhere to be found. Now, I'm not saying that other drivers in that lot could possibly have had anything to do with the disappearance of that Afghani driver but he should have known he might make somebody mad.

It was the last week of December 2001. The tragedy of the 9-11 terrorist attack was still quite fresh in our minds. We were driving north on highway 7 in Connecticut at about three o'clock in the morning. The road was nearly empty of traffic. We hadn't heard anything on the CB radio for a couple of hours and all seemed quiet except for the sounds of the truck rolling down the road and the stereo playing softly in the background. Suddenly, we heard something hit the truck and felt the truck rock sharply. We looked around but couldn't tell what had caused the truck to rock the way it did. Then we noticed the bullet hole in the windshield on the drivers' side.

It looked as though it may have been a 22-caliber slug that

hit the windshield. We saw that the bullet had not quite penetrated through all of the layers of glass and realized that if it had gone all the way through, it would have hit Don right in the face. We pulled off into a truck service plaza and called the police but they were unable to find the person who shot at us. The incident shook us up for a while but we had to go on to make our appointment.

A few weeks later, we were driving southbound on highway 71 heading toward Cincinnati, OH. It was a dark night and traffic began to get heavy as we got closer to the city. Just ahead of us, we saw a small four-wheeler pull off onto the shoulder of the road. A man got out of the car and began walking toward the oncoming traffic. We realized that he was walking into the road and appeared to be walking right into the front of our truck. At the last moment Don pulled over and avoided the man. He quickly picked up the microphone to warn drivers behind us. A driver behind us said, "Whoa, that was close! I almost hit him!" For several minutes we heard drivers behind us talking about the man. He was continuing to try to throw himself in front of a truck. Finally, we heard that a car had hit the man and that several others had been hurt and killed in the mishap.

Chapter Three
Big Boys with Big Toys

Trucks come in all shapes, sizes, styles and types. Most have manual transmissions with as many as eighteen speeds including split gears which are high and low settings on those gears. Some manufacturers are producing trucks with automatic transmissions, which are easier to drive but are considered to be less of a truck by the long time drivers, many of whom started out driving trucks with manual breaks, steering and no air conditioning.

A "one stack Mack with a window in the back", describes a Mack "day-cab" truck. Generally intended for day-time driving, day-cabs are generally "Cab-Overs" which means the cab of the truck actually sits over the engine and they don't have sleeping compartments. That's a tight squeeze for some of the larger drivers.

The next step up is a truck with a crawl-in sleeper. There is no room to stand up in a crawl-in and the driver usually has to climb over the engine to get into the sleeper, which is little larger than a coffin and has little storage space. These trucks are generally used to transport freight within a three of four state area that keeps the driver out for only two or three days.

In walk-in sleepers and studio sleepers, you can stand up

and even walk a step or two. Many walk-ins and studios are equipped with closet space, storage compartments and small refrigerators. A specially modified truck with a stretched wheel base may have a large living quarters with a sink, shower and toilet much like a self contained motor home.

There are many different models of semi-trucks on the road. Most truck manufacturers have a large line of styles ranging from day-cabs to top of the line studio sleepers and for the right price, the manufacturer will build a truck to the owners' specifications including a kitchen area, shower, toilet and much more. We saw one in Texas that had parquet flooring, plush carpeting on the walls and ceiling and a beautiful mural painted on the outside.

Of course, drivers have come up with CB slang names for the different model trucks. Frieghtliners are referred to as "Frieghtshakers." While Peterbilt trucks are called "Petercars" and Kenworth trucks are called "K Whoppers" or "Kitty Whoppers." I guess the funniest one I heard would be for Volvo. Somewhere along the way somebody found out the word "Volvo" is Swedish for penis. So now they call it a "Dick." I have heard a few drivers take a chiding… "Hey driver, are you ridin' that Dick hard?" or "Don't go strokin' that thing too fast now driver!"

Most semi-truck engines are built to pull heavy loads up to 81,000 pounds and can travel at speeds of 75 to 120 miles per hour. "Driver, I'm proceeding at a ridiculous rate of fuel consumption!" The fuel tanks on many trucks can hold 200 hundred gallons or more and get between 4½ to 6 miles per gallon. Many trucks today are equipped with pollution control devices and there is a move by manufacturers to produce cleaner burning, more efficient engines.

Many companies have their fleet trucks "castrated" by having them hooked up to a computer and adjusted so that the trucks will only run 68 miles an hour top speed before the engine shuts down. Still other companies have transponders and laptop computers on their trucks that record distance, speed and location of the trucks and allow the company dispatchers to communicate with the drivers at any given time. It's kind of like having a leash on the trucks and in fact, many drivers refer to their trucks as "Dogs." As for us, our truck has not been "castrated" and we don't have a leash.

At one point a few years ago, we owned four trucks. Don drove one of the trucks and we hired three other drivers. Now, it's hard enough to take care of one truck with all the expense of fuel, payments, tags, taxes, maintenance and upkeep plus running it enough to make a profit. But when you have several trucks, you have to find and keep good drivers who can be trusted to take good care of your truck. We found one driver who took things just a little too far.

"Bugs," as he called himself, drove one of our trucks for a while. He was a tall good-looking man with a big grin and a good driver but he spent a lot of time cleaning the truck. In fact, he wanted to wash it every two or three days. Running a big rig through a truck wash can cost anywhere from $35. to $50. or more. We would pay for two truck washes a month. The rest Bugs would pay himself. He would get up early some mornings and dry the dew off of the truck before driving down the road, which often made him late for his appointment. He would go into chrome shops and buy decorative accessories for the truck and spend so much money that he would have to call in for an advance on his check to have money to eat on. And it wasn't even his truck!

Another driver had a long-haired dog that rode with him in the truck. Now, many drivers carry dogs with them in the truck because dogs make good company but they are usually small breeds and, most of the time, the drivers are very good about stopping to walk their dogs and clean up after them. After he left us, I had to clean the truck he had been driving. As I climbed in to the truck to clean, the odor hit me. There was a thick coat of long dog hair everywhere and as I looked around I noticed a small brown pile on the floor of the sleeper. Apparently the driver neglected to walk his dog on a regular basis.

Most of the drivers that we hired were pretty good fellows for the most part but it's difficult for a small owner/operator to compete with big companies for drivers. We were lucky to find a few local drivers but we couldn't keep them for long. A large company can offer drivers a good percentage or salary plus low cost insurance and retirement plans with group rates but a man who owns only a few trucks can't afford to offer his drivers much more than a job.

The majority of drivers work for large trucking companies that have dispatchers who coordinate loads to get them from one place to another. The company pays the driver in a company truck either a percentage of what the load pays or a flat cent per mile rate. The company will also pay for truck tags, insurance, maintenance, fuel and tolls. A driver who owns his own truck leases in with a company and will be paid a larger percentage or mileage rate but has to pay for his own tags, insurance, maintenance, fuel and tolls. The trucking company generally furnishes the trailers although an owner/operator may have his own trailer and is paid a little more for its use. Either way, the company usually makes most of the money.

The company may have its own product to ship out or the dispatcher might call a broker who has access to multiple companies and loads across the country. A driver in south Florida might load oranges going to Virginia. Then he will call his dispatcher who will send him to pick up a load in Baltimore, Maryland which is bound for Ohio. The dispatcher will look for loads coming out of Ohio going to one of the company plants in Texas. From there, the driver will probably go right back to Florida. We have loaded peanuts to Texas from Georgia only to turn right around and load peanuts going back to Georgia.

Our truck is a Kenworth and has a large studio sleeper. It's pretty big inside and has a couch that folds out to make a bed. Some trucks are equipped with very large interiors and have toilets, showers, and kitchen areas. That's the kind of truck a driver can live in! Some drivers dress their trucks up and compete in national truck competitions. The fancier trucks are decorated with elaborate paint jobs, murals, "chicken lights" or auxiliary lights and as many chrome accessories as possible. Some drivers put large train horns on their trucks. Talk about all the bells and whistles! "Yeah driver, I'm styling and profiling, looking ever so cool sitting on the stool of my store-bought large car! 10-4?"

There are all kinds of trailers being pulled behind those trucks. The most familiar so probably the "Dry Box" is used for hauling dry durable goods like furniture, canned goods and other materials for manufacturing and retail. Refrigerated trailers have on-board cooling systems that can be set at the desired temperature for the products being shipped. Produce is often hauled in a refrigerated trailer and they are often called "Garbage Wagons."

"Covered Wagons" are open-top trailers, which are used to transport grain, wood chips or other loose dry material. These trailers are supposed to be covered with tarps when they are loaded to prevent loose materials from flying out onto the road. Flat bed trailers are just that, flat open trailers. Often, the freight has to be strapped down and tarped to secure and protect it from the weather. Log truck trailers are "Flat Beds" with support poles along the side of the trailer. The logs are generally strapped down but one can't be too careful about driving around them.

"Drop Decks," "Double Drops," and "Skate Boards" describe open trailers with different levels. A "Drop Deck" has two levels, the "Doubled Drop" has three levels like stairs and the "Skate Board" has three levels; the first one drops down to the second level and back up to the third. There are stretched out versions of these trailers that are designed to haul large pieces of industrial equipment and generally have to have an escort on the road because of their large size.

Sometimes you'll see trucks pulling two or three "Dry Box" trailers hooked together in tandem. Also called "Wiggle Wagons," they are a little more difficult to pull, maneuver and almost impossible to back up. It's best to be especially careful when driving around "Wiggle Wagons." They were given that name for a good reason.

Mobile home movers or "Shanty Shakers" are only allowed to move during daylight hours. They transport 14' to 16' wide mobile home components. They are generally escorted down the highway due to the width of the mobile homes and will have banners or signs on the trucks that say "Oversized Load." "Shanty Shakers" are also called "Mobile Modular Residential Commercial Transportation Relocation Technical Specialist." That is a mouthful to say on the CB.

Another type of trailer is the "Parking Lot." These trailers are designed to haul cars, trucks and vans. Some will be taken to car lots but many of the cars belong to "Snow Birds" who move north or south according to the weather and have their vehicles transported to summer or winter homes. It can be a lucrative business just moving cars for "Snow Birds" for a driver with his own "Parking Lot."

Trucks can be driven by a single driver or by a team. A driver can log up to ten hours of driving time per day. Some companies employ teams of two drivers who can keep trucks in motion trading off driving time. It can be difficult to be in a truck with someone for long periods at a time. The cab of a truck is a small place and a team of two drivers has to be able to get along together in the truck for days or weeks at a time.

Man and wife teams are very common these days. One lady we know quit her job working in a local shop and went to a large trucking company who put her through driving school for three weeks. After she got her license, her husband went to the school, got his license and got into the truck with his wife. Now, they drive across the country together.

Chapter Four
Bears

"Lovingly" referred to as "Bears" because they tend to hide behind bushes while scanning radar for speeders; the law enforcement officers of this country have a dangerous and difficult job. Although most drivers appreciate the need for law enforcement and don't like getting caught by the bears, they sure wouldn't want to be out on the road without them.

Bears are an obstacle to avoid and a main staple for trucker slang. They have been given a number of cute names such as "City Kitties," "Local Yokels," "County Mounties," "Super Troopers," "Care Bears," "Bears in the air," "Boy Scouts," "She Bears," "Hunney Bears," "Bears on Four Legs" and "Crotch Rocket Cops". These are some of the nicer names that drivers use to describe police officers.

"City Kitties" and "Local Yokels" are local city police and usually don't patrol interstate highways. However they can station themselves at on and off ramps with radar guns.

"Break one nine, northbound. You've got a city kitty shootin' you in the back at the 15."

"Yeah, driver, they must be trying to raise Krispy Kream money."

"County Mounties" are county sheriff's deputies who patrol

county streets and highways. County Mounties have a little more authority and can patrol larger areas than city police. They also work as backup for state and local law enforcement.

"Super Troopers" are state police. They patrol the highways and are available to help support local, city and county law enforcement. While "City Kitties," "County Mounties," and "Super Troopers" are fully capable of pulling over a big rig, their authority only goes so far. They can give a driver a speeding ticket or other moving violation but they don't have the automatic right to look at the logbook or search the truck. That's where the DOT (Department of Transportation) officer comes in.

A state DOT officer, or "sure 'nough full grown bear," generally checks for safety violations. His inspection might include the overall condition of the rig and trailer, cargo, weight, tire condition, lights, breaks, logbooks, and even the driver himself if he thinks the driver may be driving under an impaired condition. At which point the officer can administer a "Whiz Quiz" or drug test. That's what they mean by "Checkin' your chickens."

The DOT has the authority to check the logbook, the truck and or the driver himself to for any potential violation. However, if the driver believes that he is being unfairly stopped or ticketed, he can call the federal marshal or "Big Dog" to resolve the problem although that is no guarantee that the driver won't get a ticket.

"Care Bears" can be local, county or state police who sit in and around construction sites to provide protection for road workers and prevent or catch speeders and other law breakers. Sometimes they just leave empty patrol cars with their lights flashing in these areas. It's hard to tell whether or not the patrol car is empty so it's a pretty effective deterrent.

"Bears in the air" refers to officers in helicopters. Also known as "Eyes in the sky," they generally fly over high traffic areas to watch for speeders and "aggressive drivers." The other extreme is an officer on horseback or "Bear on Four Legs" and also motorcycle officers or "Crotch Rocket Cops." Police in unmarked cars are called "Plain Wrappers."

"You got a "Plain red Wrapper" at the 35. He's flashin' and dashin' in the hammer lane coming up behind you southbound."

Oh, and let's not forget the "Hunney Bears" and "She Bears" who are female officers. However, there is a distinction between the two. "She Bears" are just regular female officers but the "Hunney Bear" is an *attractive* female officer. Don't let the fact that they are females fool you. They can pull you over and give you a ticket as well as any male officer can.

"Feeding the bears" or getting speeding tickets is very common for truck drivers. Most drivers who get a ticket usually deserve them though; there are some exceptions. Drivers are often in a hurry and the bears are out there watching for them. The best thing for a driver who gets ticketed frequently, whether they deserve it or not, is to find a lawyer in the county where he got the ticket and have the lawyer "work out a deal" with the judge. Generally, they will reduce the charge and impose a small fine. Paying a lawyer may seem costly for a speeding ticket but it will keep points off of a driver's license. Ether way...the driver pays.

When I met Don, he already had a long history of getting speeding tickets. It seemed that I was sending fines off every week or so. I looked closely at his right shoe to see if there were any lead weights in it. It didn't do any good to fuss at him about it. He was just trying to get where he was suppose to be when he was supposed to be there. He has had to take a defensive driving course a time or two in order to keep the points off of his license. He tries to avoid tickets and has gotten better about speeding these days.

Sometimes drivers will "Shake the bushes."

A northbound driver is in a hurry. "How about ya' southbound, what did you leave behind you?"

"You got a local yokel shootin' you in the back at the 25 and some care bears in the destruction zone at the 58, northbound. The chicken coops were closed when I came through."

"Preeshaydit, southbound. I'm traveling at a ridiculous rate of fuel consumption and I ain't seen nothin' back that away."

Accidents or "incidents" as they are generally referred to, are the biggest concern for anyone on the road. The October 2002 issue of *Land Line* magazine quotes a statistic from an AAA Foundation study which shows that 98 percent of driver fatalities in car-truck crashes are primarily because of the differences in the size of the vehicles. About 80 percent of the car drivers had at least one unsafe driving act recorded compared to 27 percent of truck drivers. Each driver could have up to four unsafe driving acts recorded and if you look at all of these unsafe actions, 75 percent were linked to car drivers and 25 percent were linked to truck drivers.

I can understand why the statistics point toward the difference in size as being a primary cause for accidents. As I ride in the passenger seat of this big truck, I see small cars slip up alongside and disappear in front of the truck. Then all I could see was the tip of the radio antenna. That is a bad place for a car to be especially if there is a sudden stop. A truck driving 55 MPH can take 100 feet or more to come to a complete stop. The general rule of thumb if you are in a car is if you can't see the driver in the truck or in his mirrors, he can't see you.

A common mistake that car drivers make is trying to make a right hand turn by a truck that is also making a right hand turn.

Almost all trailers display a sign on the back the reads, "This Truck Makes Wide Turns." Semi-trucks must make a wide swing into the intersection to make right turns. We were riding behind a truck turning right at an intersection and watched as the driver of a nice BMW pull up into the turning lane just as the truck was swinging around to make his turn. For the driver, it was too late. The back wheels of the trailer rolled all over the hood of the car. Fortunately, no one was hurt but the driver of the BMW learned a hard lesson that day.

Another thing that drivers have to deal with is the logbook. Often referred to a "comic book," the logbook is a detailed record of the drivers' time on the road. A driver is only suppose to drive a total of ten hours driving time before he has to stop and go into the sleeper. Ninety percent of the records in the average logbook is a total lie. All too often, a driver can't make his appointment in the time allotted. He either has to lie in the logbook or miss his appointment, which means he will probably miss the next load out and that means losing money. However, if he gets caught falsifying a logbook, the DOT (Department of transportation) officer, or "sure enough full-grown bear," will write a big ticket with fines that start at about $1000. Then the officer will check out the truck and write tickets for anything that isn't up to standards. That driver will end up paying thousands of dollars in fines before he's through.

Just south of Donalson, Georgia; on Highway 84 is a stretch of road, which has been patrolled for more than a decade by a bear who goes by the handle "Speed Buggy." There is a crude hand-made sign on the side of the road about a mile ahead of his patrol area that reads "Speed Trap!" The speed limit drops quickly from 65 to 45 miles an hour in the next mile. Then, just over the hill, he waits for his next victim. Many truck drivers have been pulled over by "Speed Buggy" and he has earned a reputation for being relentless in his pursuit of speeders. His son has since joined the force and the drivers are calling him "Speed Buggy, Jr.," although I don't think he appreciates the handle much.

"Break one nine. How about ya' eastbound, What did you leave behind you?"

"Westbound, you got bears wall to wall in the next fifteen miles. The chicken coops are open for business and they are checkin' your chickens so, you might want to catch your comic book up."

Personally, I never even notice weigh stations or "chicken coops" before I got into this truck. Most states have them stationed near state lines and there are mobile units that can be set up anywhere on the road.

There are laws that govern the CB radio. The FCC or Federal Communications Commission ("Friendly Candy Company") is an independent US government agency, directly responsible to Congress and is charged with regulating interstate and international communications by radio, television, wire, satellite and cable. At first, users were required to obtain a CB radio license and call letters from the FCC to operate a CB radio. However, the FCC was flooded with requests for CB radio licenses that they finally abandoned formal licensing and allowed operators to buy CB radio equipment and go on the air without any license or call letters.

Although no license is required to operate a CB radio, FCC Laws Part 95, Subpart D, which contains the FCC's rules for CB radio operation, are still in effect. These rules cover CB radio equipment, the ban on linear amplifiers, and the types of communications permitted on the air. Despite the FCC rules and regulations, drivers find ways to obtain linear amplifiers and other equipment to increase out-put on their radios.

CB radio channel 9 may be used only for emergency communications or for traveler's assistance. The Radio Emergency Associated Communications Teams (REACT) is a non-profit public service organization comprised of volunteers throughout the United States who monitor channel 9. They do an excellent job of guarding CB Radio Channel 9 specifically for emergencies or requests for directions. Its members can take advantage of REACT headquarters programs, which include group insurance, conventions, team newsletters, and special CB Radio equipment discounts.

Trucker Buddy is a non-profit organization dedicated to educating and mentoring school children about the trucking industry. Trucker Buddy matches up professional truck drivers with classes of children in grades 2-8. The drivers develop relationships as pen-pals with the children writing them weekly with news about their travels and provide a format for the enhancement of the grade school curriculum in reading, writing, geography, mathematics, social studies and history. Since 1992, Trucker Buddy has helped to educate over a half million school children and introduce them to a caring, compassionate group of men and women, the nations' professional truck drivers.

Along most of I75 in Georgia just south of Atlanta, Georgia, the third lane is restricted to big trucks. We were in the second lane and noticed a car "four wheeler" about to come onto the road from an off ramp. There were trucks and cars in both the right lane and middle lanes so we pulled over to the third lane to allow the other vehicles to pull over and give the driver of the four wheeler to come safely onto the road. We tried to get back out of the third lane as quickly as we could but it took some time for the other drivers to make room for us and while we were trying to get over, we noticed a City Kitty with his "gum ball machine" flashing behind us.

We pulled over to the side of the road and Don got out to talk with the officer. I could see him in the rear view mirror and I could tell he was getting upset as he tried to explain what happened. A few moments later, Don and the officer walked up to my side of the truck and Don asked me for the registration card from the glove box. I could hear him cussing that officer saying that he was only trying to avoid an accident. I could see the officers' face as he listened to what Don had to say but he continued to write the ticket. I prayed that Don would calm down. I was afraid that he might be arrested. Finally the officer said, "Sir, if you'll just let me finish writing this out, I'll get out of your way!"

We went to court about that ticket thinking that we could simply explain the circumstances to the judge and that he might understand and make an exception in our case. What a joke! Court was held in a broken down old school house cafeteria. The judges' bench was a large piece of plywood laying across an old table. There were only about five cases being heard that morning and ours was the last. We noticed that there were about six officers that came into the room just before our case was to be heard. I thought to myself, in a town as small as Byron, Georgia is, this must be their entire police force in that courtroom.

When our case was called, the officers all gathered around behind us. We explained the situation to the judge but he acted as though we hadn't said anything at all. Finally, he ruled guilty and set the fine at $91.50. We asked the judge to please try to keep the points off of Dons' license but he started talking to one of the officers, totally ignoring us.

Infuriated, Don left the courtroom saying that this must be one of them "kangaroo" courts and I stayed to pay the fine. I saw several of the officers follow him out and watch as he got into his truck. After I paid the fine, all except the 50 cents because the clerk didn't have change, I went through the kitchen of the old cafeteria and out the back door. As I walked back to the truck, I turned around and noticed the officers as they poked their heads around the corner one by one. They watched us until we left the parking lot. It was then that we realized that they must have thought that Don was going to cause a problem and they might need to restrain him. After that incident, we decided to just hire local lawyers to handle these things. It's expensive but better than the headaches.

Chapter Five
Truck Stops and Pickle Parks

There are hundreds of truck stops across America. Many years ago, the few truck stops along the road were small, dirty and offered little comfort to drivers. These days they range in size from simple roadside fuel stops and truck service centers to full service truck stops, which are more like shopping malls. Some of the larger truck stops include convenience stores, hotel rooms, restaurants, showers, barber shops, laundromats, movie theaters and much more. I have even heard that Wal-Mart has its own truck stop in Virginia. Although I understand it's just a Wal-Mart that allows truck drivers to park in their lot, I still can't wait to see that one. OK, I'll admit it. I am a Wal-Mart junkie.

Most truck stops have large parking lots and in most cases, the parking is free. A driver, who is laid over for one reason or another, can park his truck in one of these lots for a few hours, days or even weeks at a time. Pulling a big rig through the lot, a driver locates a space he can get into and depending one how experienced he is, he might back right into that space or it might take him two or three tries.

"How bout you driver? You need some help backin' up that big truck?"

"Yeah, he needs to spray some Pam on the sides of that thing so he can slide it on in there, Roger?"

"Maybe you'd like to come show me how driver!"

"Somebody needs to show you something!"

"Damn! That 'juvenile delinquent' just tore the bumper off my truck."

After a nap, a driver can go into the truck stop to get a bite to eat. Eating at truck stop cafés can be a little like playing Russian Roulette. Sometimes, the food is great and you try to remember where those places are but sometimes what you get is overcooked, undercooked or just plain rotten. Don and I have seen our fair share of food poisoning and I can tell you from personal experience: There is nothing more miserable than being sick while your riding down the road. After eating some bad hash browns in Memphis, TN, I was bent over a trash bucket throwing up and wondering if I was going to need a bucket for my other end!

We have a refrigerator, microwave and coffeepot in our truck along with a satellite dish and TV with VCR. We keep the truck stocked with food and generally eat hot sandwiches, soups and other microwave dishes on the road. However, it's nice to have a good hot meal once in a while. So, we keep our eyes peeled for a good truck stop café. We were sitting at a booth in one of these truck stop cafés when we heard the desk clerk announce over the intercom system, "J B Hunt, party of five, your shower is ready!"

Many truck stops have showers with full-time attendants who clean the shower rooms and restock them with soap and paper. Sometimes you have to leave a deposit for the towels but you can get extra towels if you ask for them. Don and I share a shower and we generally ask the desk clerk for a shower for two. Some the better truck stops have nice large shower rooms with dual shower heads, heat lamps and hair dryers installed but we've been in a few that were so small, you'd have to go outside to change your mind! We have squeezed two people into a space barely big enough for one and managed to wash the day off so we could get back on the road.

Many truck stops offer TV and telephone hook up services for a small fee so drivers can watch TV and stay in touch with their families. Or, the driver might decide to go inside to the video arcade to pass the time. Some of these places have slot machines as well as a variety of money eating gaming and vending machines. While he's there, the driver can get his haircut, have his boots shined and talk to other drivers while he washes and dries his clothes. After a while, he'll go back to his truck and turn on the CB radio to listen to the chatter.

"Commercial company on 23," a female voice called.

"Commercial company?" I asked as Don sat down on the couch in the back of the cab.

"That's a lot lizard," he began, "they also call them recreational reptiles."

Now I was confused.

"What's a lot lizard?" I asked.

"A lot lizard is a prostitute who works in truck stop parking lots," he said.

"And she's advertising on channel 23?" I asked.

"Yes," he said, "they generally use channel 23."

Out of curiosity, I turned to channel 23 and listened. "You there commercial?" a man's voice asked.

"You got Sunshine here!" a female voice answered.

"What's your twenty Sunshine?" the driver asked.

"I'm back here on the party row. Where are you?" she replied. I found out that the party row is generally the last row of parking spaces in a truck stop and that's where the lot lizards hang out, although they will go anywhere on the lot to "work."

"I'm back here on the party row in a green Pete," he said.

"What are you looking for tonight driver?" she asked.

"Whatever I can get!" he said.

"OK, I'll be over there in a few minutes. 10-4?" A few moments later, we saw a young woman walk across the parking lot toward the back row where she knocked on the door of one of the trucks.

Prostitution is actually legal in a few places like Las Vegas where it has become a regulated tax paying industry. But, for most of the country it is still alive, well and illegal not only on dimly lit street corners in the big cities but in the trucking business as well. In some states, if a man is caught taking the services of a prostitute, that state will send a copy of the arrest warrant to the driver's home address. We heard one driver on the CB telling another that he sure hoped that he got home before the "old lady" saw that paper.

I turned the CB back to 19 to see what else might be going on. Along with the usual conversations about who has what load and where they are going, I heard a driver trying to sell some tools and another one trying to sell videos. I looked back at Don and asked, "They are selling those things pretty cheap aren't they?"

"Yeah, they call that 'singing a sonnet.' They're probably broke and trying to raise a little cash but some drivers sell stuff like radio equipment, chrome polish or even drugs over the CB as a sideline to make extra money."

A few minutes later I heard a couple of drivers talking. "How bout' ya, Spanky. You got your ears on?"

"This is Spanky. Come on."

"This is Bootleg. Is that you by that 'Ballet Dancer'?"

"Yeah, he's got commercial company in there and they've

been at it for a while now." I could see the truck they were talking about. The antenna of that truck swayed wildly back and forth. I can understand why they called it a "Ballet dancer."

It was about two in the morning. Don and I were sleeping in the bunk when suddenly there was a loud knock on the door of the cab. Don got up to look out the window. He rolled the window down and women's voice said, "Do you need some company tonight driver?"

"No," he said "I've got my wife in here with me."

"Well, does she want some company tonight?" she asked. Don looked over to me and I shook my head no and laughed.

"She must be one of those full service lot lizards," I said.

"Well, let me know if you change your mind," she said. "Just call for Precious on channel 23."

We pulled into a truck stop in Elkton, Maryland one late spring afternoon and laid down to take a nap. About the time we had gotten to sleep, we heard a loud knock on the door of the truck. Don got up to see who it was. When he opened the window, a female voice asked if she could come in out of the cold. It was about 70 degrees that day but Don, half asleep, told the woman to come in. She sat in the passenger seat and started talking to Don about the problems she and her husband were having trying to raise money for the trip home. I turned over to see what was going on. When she looked back into the sleeper and saw me, she quickly said that she had made a mistake and jumped out of the truck.

Don and I were both a little confused about our visitor. If she was trying to help her husband raise money, why did she stop and jump out of the truck when she saw me? We decided that she couldn't be a lot lizard because we were parked in a secure lot with a chain link fence and security guards who don't allow lot lizards or anyone who isn't in a truck onto the lot. We wondered if she was in fact an undercover cop trying to catch drivers who might employ commercial company.

An alternative to the truck stop is the rest area. Generally referred to as a "Pickle Park," the average rest area has little more than a parking place, a bathroom, telephone and vending machines. We've encountered a few homeless people at some of these Pickle Parks. One young couple whose car had broke down had camped out at the rest area. We watched as the young woman dressed in a tight pair of short shorts walked over to a water spigot with her towel and shampoo in hand. She bent over holding her head under the water. I watched several drivers in nearby trucks pressing their noses against their windshields as she bent low with her back to them. It was as though she was deliberately putting on a show for those drivers. After a few minutes, one of the drivers walked up to the young woman and began talking to her. A short time later, they both walked back to his truck. "I guess she was advertising wasn't she?" I asked. Don just nodded.

There are many rest areas that have no facilities. These rest areas are often called "peter pleasing pickle parks" because bisexual and homosexual men often hang around them looking for sex partners. We pulled into one of these so-called "peter pleasing pickle parks" late one afternoon to take a nap.

As I hung the curtain on the windshield, I noticed that a small car parked in front of us was flashing his parking lights. I turned and asked Don, "Do you think that man needs help?"

Don turned to me smiling as he said, "Oh, yes, he needs help all right, but not the kind of help you're thinking about." A few moments later, another truck pulled into the parking lot and once again the driver of the little four-wheeler flashed his parking lights. Then I noticed that the truck driver was flashing his parking lights. They flashed their parking lights at each other a couple of times and then the driver of the four-wheeler got out of his car and walked into the nearby woods. Minutes later, the truck driver got out of his truck and followed the young man into the woods.

I saw the same scene repeated a couple more times. Each time the young man would flash his lights at the cars or trucks pulling into the rest area. A willing driver would flash his lights back to the man in the four-wheeler, then get out of his car, and walk the same path into the woods.

After watching the young man go back into the wood a few times I said, "That man has gone back into the woods several times now. He must have eaten something bad."

Don said, "No, he's doing something else back there."

"What do you mean?" I asked.

"Do you see the drivers following him into the woods?" he asked.

"Yes!" I said. I was a little naïve about this sort of thing at the time. After a moment I asked, "Are they doing what I think they are doing?"

He turned to me and nodded as he said, "He's washing weenies back there."

"Washing weenies?" I asked.

He nodded again. "You mean that they are performing sexual favors for each other?" I asked.

"Yep! He's a sidewalk weenie washer," he said with a smile.

I noticed another four-wheeler pull up into the parking lot and start flashing his parking lights. They seemed like well-dressed young men and I could see a car seat in the back seat of one of the cars. I wondered if these men were married and had children. "They come here after work to satisfy their sexual needs and then go home to their families and friends." Don started as he crawled into the bunk. "They lead a secret life out here."

Occasionally we find a small café or Bar-B-Que place that has truck parking. We had just eaten at one such place and had crawled back into the truck when we noticed a young black woman crawling out from under a trailer parked nearby. She quickly ran over to a nearby car and jumped into the passenger's seat. We watched as the car sped out of the parking lot and down the street. Moments later, a driver came around the side of the truck that the woman had crawled under. He went quickly around the lot looking back and forth but she was long gone. Don chuckled and said, "I bet that lizard just got his wallet!"

I smiled and said, "Well, I guess 'lizards' can be hazardous in more ways than one!"

Riding down the highway, I pick up my guitar and strum a tune. As I keep time with the beat of the truck and harmonize with the hum of the engine, I realize that the truck has a rhythm all it's own…the rhythm of the road itself. The story doesn't end here because every time I get into the cab of the truck, I find something new or different. The adventure has educated and inspired me and I hope that my story has done the same for you. "Eight's and Eight's" Ya'll. 10-4?

Chapter Six
Jokes

Long hours of monotonous driving can make any driver sleepy and drivers often listen to the CB to help them stay awake. Most of what's heard on the CB is dull conversation between drivers about their destination, traffic or other truck drivers but occasionally you hear a joke or two. The following are some of the jokes I've collected from various sources.

A driver has a CB radio in his truck but it's a "Mud duck" and doesn't work very well so, he buys himself another one. When he keys up his mike, he's steppin' on drivers for miles around. But, he's not satisfied so he has the new radio souped up tweaked out and installs a high powered antenna. When he keys up the mike, lightening bolts shoot from the antenna. He yells, "Oh God!" A small voice comes back on the radio, "Come in!"

What's the difference between a truck drivers boots and cowboy boots? Cowboy boots have the bullshit on the outside.

Driving down the road to make his delivery, a driver sees four naked old women laying on the grass in front of a retirement home. He thought it was kind of unusual but continued on to deliver his load. On his way back through town, he sees the same four old naked women lying on the grass in front of the retirement home. This time he decides to stop. He goes into the building and asks the director, "Do you know you've got four naked old women laying on the grass out front?"

The director turns to him and says, "Yes, they are retired prostitutes and they are trying to have a yard sale."

Why aren't truckers allowed at McDonalds any more? They keep getting hurt on the playground equipment.

A truck driver was driving along on the freeway. A sign comes up that reads "low bridge ahead." He tries to turn off but, before he knows it, the bridge is right there and he gets stuck under it. Cars are backed up for miles. Finally, a police car comes up. The cop gets out of his car and walks around to the truck driver, puts his hands on his hips and says, "Got stuck huh?"

The truck driver says, "No, I was delivering this bridge and ran out of gas"

Three truckers die and go to heaven, they are standing in front of St. Peter. St. Peter says "Oh Man I made a big mistake, you guys weren't supposed to be here yet. Tell you what, you guys can go back and be whatever you want to be."

56

The first driver says he wants to be a movie star, because they are pampered. St. Peter says "Ok, go ahead and jump and yell MOVIE STAR on your way down. So the first driver does.

The second driver says he wants to be a race car driver, he likes to drive fast. St. Peter tells him to go ahead and do the same thing and yell RACE CAR DRIVER as he jumps.

Now comes the third fellow, he wants to be a BOUNTY HUNTER. St. Peter says go ahead and jump. While running for the door the guy trips, on the way down he is yelling "OH! SHIT!"

A trucker comes home to find his wife rubbing her boobs with lemon, he asks, "What on earth are you doing?"

She says, "I heard if you rub em with lemon, they get bigger."

He says, "Well, then why don't you use toilet paper?"

"Toilet paper?" she asks.

He says, "Yeah, you've been wiping your butt with it all these years, and look how big it's gotten..."

The greatest truck driver in the world was driving along a country lane late one night when his truck broke down. All he could see was a faint light in the distance, so he headed towards it. He came to an old farmhouse and knocked on the door. "Hello," he says, "I'm the greatest truck driver in the world and my truck has broken down. I wonder could I have a bed for the night?"

"Well," says the farmer, "there's only two rooms, myself and the wife in one, and my young daughter in the other."

"Look, I'm the greatest truck driver in the world and all I want is a bed for the night, your daughter will be as safe as a house," says the greatest truck driver in the world.

"Okay," says the farmer, and they all went to bed. At four in the morning, the farmer hears the headboard next door banging against the wall. He got up, looked in, and there was the greatest truck driver in the world driving it into his daughter, with his bare ass going up and down. The farmer went downstairs and loaded the shotgun. He snuck into the room and shoved the shotgun up the greatest truck driver in the world's butt. "Okay," he says, "if you're the greatest truck driver in the world, try and reverse out of there with a full load!"

What is the difference between a well mannered, non-sexist, male truck driver and The Yeti? There is a small chance that The Yeti exists!

They say truck drivers like fat girls because when they bend over their ass looks like a fifth wheel. They just want to hook up!

A truck driver who had been delivering radioactive waste for the local reactor begins to feel sick after a few years on the job. He decided to seek compensation for his ailment. Upon his arrival at the workers' compensation department, he his interviewed by an assessor.

Assessor: I see you work with radio-active materials and wish to claim compensation.

Trucker: Yeah, I feel really sick.

Assessor: All right then, does your employer take measures to protect you from radiation poisoning?

Trucker: Yeah, he gives me a lead suit to wear on the job.
Assessor: And what about the cabin in which you drive?
Trucker: Oh yeah. That's lead lined, all lead lined.
Assessor: What about the waste itself? Where is that kept?
Trucker: Oh, the stuff is held in a lead container, all lead.
Assessor: Let me see if I get this straight. You wear a lead suit, sit in a lead-lined cabin and the radioactive waste is kept in a lead container.
Trucker: Yeah, that's right. All lead.
Assessor: Then I can't see how you could claim against him for radiation poisoning.
Trucker: I'm not. I claiming for lead poisoning.

1st. Lady Truck Driver: "If men are suppose to be the more efficient, hard-working, and reliable of the two sexes then why do they name their pride & joy trucks after women."
2nd. Lady Trucker Driver: "Oh that's easy. You see, if she is fit and well he can just sit on his backside and enjoy the ride as she carries him and his load everywhere. But if she has a breakdown through lack of maintenance and too much hard-work he can kick her and blame her for all of his troubles. Of course, all of the time he will be keeping his eyes open for a younger, sleeker model."

A 72-year-old man goes to his wife and tells her he plans to go to the doctor to get some Viagra. She drops what she's doing and heads for the door. He asks her, "Where do you think you're going?"
She says, "I'm going to get a tetanus shot if you're going to get that rusty old thing up."

One driver asks another, "Is there a restaurant where you can eat up at this truck stop?" The other driver responds, "No, it's just a restaurant."

A truck driver pulled over to the side of the road and picked up two homosexuals who were hitchhiking. They climbed into the cab and the truck driver pulled the rig back onto the highway. A few minutes later, the first fag said. "Excuse me, but I have to fart." He held his breath, then the truck driver heard a low "Hsssssss."

A few miles down the road, the second fag announced, "Excuse me, but I have to fart." The announcement was followed by another low "Hsssssss."

"Christ!" the truck driver exclaimed. "You fairies can't even fart like men. Listen to this." A moment later he emitted a deafening staccato machine gun burst from his arse.

"Ohhh!" one fag exclaimed, turning to the other. "You know what we have here, Bruce? A real virgin!"

A truck driver was driving down the highway when he saw a priest at the side of the road. He stopped to pick up the priest and give him a ride. A ways down the road the truck driver saw a lawyer on the side of the road. He turned the truck on a direct course toward the lawyer. Then he thought "Oh no, I have a priest in the truck I can't run down this lawyer!" At the last second the truck driver swerved to miss the lawyer but, the driver heard a thump outside of the truck. He looked in his rear-view mirror but didn't see anything. He turned to the priest and said "Sorry Father, I just missed that lawyer at the side of the road."

The priest said "Don't worry son, I got him with my door."

I use to think that my daddy ate light bulbs because every night I could hear him tell momma: "Turn off that light and I'll eat that thing."

A truck driver was pulled over by a state trooper. The patrolman asked him to get out of the truck and noticed the driver appeared to be putting something in his mouth as he stepped out of the cab. Figuring that the driver must be trying to hide illegal drugs, the Patrolman asked "Did I just see you swallow something?"

"Yep, that was my birth control pill," said the driver.

"Birth control pill?" asked the patrolman.

The driver said, "Yep, when I saw your lights, I knew I was screwed."

What's the difference between a male truck driver and a female truck driver?

A male truck driver will think he is the safest & best driver on the road. A female truck driver simply knows she is!

When the driver of a huge trailer lost control of his rig, he plowed into an empty tollbooth and smashed it to pieces. He climbed down from the wreckage and within a matter of minutes, a truck pulled up and discharged a crew of workers.

The men picked up each broken piece of the former tollbooth and spread some kind of creamy subsance on it. Then they began fitting the pieces together. In less than a half hour, they had the entire tollbooth reconstructed and looking good as new. "Astonishing!" the truck driver said to the crew chief. "What was the white stuff you used to get all the pieces together?"

The crew chief said, "Oh, that was tollgate booth paste."

On a sunny summer afternoon, a truck driver and his pet parrot "Petey" are cruising cross-country in their semi. Suddenly, the trucker spies a hot young girl walking along the road. He immediately pulls his truck to the side of the road. "Do you need a ride?" he asks.

"Yeah," says the girl, climbing anxiously into the truck. As they're progressing down the highway, the trucker asks the girl if she'd like to get in the back and screw. "Hell no!" says the girl.

"Well," says the truck driver as he pulls his truck to the side, "No screw, no ride." He abruptly kicks the girl out of his rig.

A short while later, the driver spots another fine teenage girl along the roadside. Again he offers a ride, and again his offer is accepted graciously. After a while, the truck driver asks the girl if she'd like to get in the back and screw. "Not for my life!" says the girl.

"Well," says the driver, "No screw, no ride." He pulls over and tells the girl to get out.

Before long, the trucker spies a third teenage cutie along the roadside. He offers her a ride and she accepts. A few miles go by and the trucker decides to try his luck again. "Do you want to get in the back and screw?" he says.

"Sure! Let's do it!" replies the girl. At this point, the trucker takes Petey and puts him in the trailer with his cargo. He then proceeds to make mad love to the woman in his cab. Upon finishing the deed, the girl says that she doesn't really need to go any farther. This is fine with the trucker, so he lets her out and continues down the road.

Before long, he starts to get a really guilty conscience about what he did. "What if that girl reports me???" he thinks to himself. No sooner did that thought cross his mind when he noticed a police cruiser behind him with its lights flashing and sirens blaring. "Oh great," the trucker thinks to himself, "maybe she did report me."

"What's the problem officer?" says the truck driver to the policeman.

"No problem really, other than the fact that you're losing your cargo out the back door... I just thought I'd let you know."

"Oh shoot!" says the truck driver upon realizing that he forgot to bring Petey back up front. The trucker and the cop walk around to the back of the trailer, and sure enough, there's Petey... throwing the frozen chicken cargo out of the back while cawing, "NO SCREW, NO RIDE!"

What goes Vroom, Screech, Vroom, Screech, Vroom, Screech?
A new truck driver at a flashing yellow light.

There was this truck driver who had to deliver 500 penguins to the state zoo. As he was driving his truck through the desert, his truck breaks down. After about 3 hours, he waves another truck down and offers the driver $500 to take these penguins to the state zoo for him. The next day the original truck driver arrives in town and sees the new truck driver crossing the road with 500 penguins walking in single file behind him. The original truck driver jumps out of his truck and asks, "What's going on? I gave you $500 to take these penguins to the zoo!"

The new truck driver responds, "I did take them to the zoo. And I had enough money left over so now we're going to see a movie."

There once was a very happy truck driver that was eating in a diner at night. Three motorcyclists came and proceeded to pick on the truck driver by pouring pepper and salt all over him, spitting in his coffee, and stealing his food. The truck driver didn't do anything. He just stood up, paid his check, and left the diner. "That truck driver sure ain't much of a fighter," said one of the cyclists.

The girl behind the counter, peering out into the night, added, "He doesn't seem like much of a driver either. He just ran his truck right over three motorcycles."

A young man at his first job as a waiter in a diner has a large trucker sit down at the counter and order, "Give me three flat tires and a couple of headlights."

Bewildered, he goes to the kitchen and tells the cook, "I think this guy's in the wrong store, look at what he ordered!"

The cook says, "He wants three pancakes and two eggs sunny-side up."

The waiter takes a bowl of beans to the trucker. He looks down and growls, "What's this? I didn't order this!"

The young man tells him, "The cook says that while you're

waiting for your parts, you might as well gas up!"

What's the difference between a puppy and a truck driver? After six months, the puppy quits whining.

There was this little guy sitting inside a bar, just looking at his drink. After he didn't move for a half-an-hour, this big trouble-making truck driver stepped up right next to him, took the drink from the guy, and just drank it all down. The poor man started crying. The truck driver turned and said: "Come on man, I was just joking. Here, I'll buy you another drink. I just can't stand to see a man crying."

"No, it's not that," the man replied. "Today is the worst day of my life. First, I overslept and was late for an important meeting. My boss became outraged and then fired me. When I left the building to my car, I found out that it was stolen. The police said they could do nothing. I then got a cab to return home, and after I paid the cab driver and the cab had gone, I found that I left my whole wallet in the cab. I got home only to find my wife was in bed with the gardener." The man was really sobbing now, "I left home depressed and came to this bar. And now, just as I was thinking about putting an end to my life, YOU show up and drink my poison!"

There was a blonde and she just got a new car. She was driving down the highway when she drove in front of a truck and ran it off the road. The truck driver got out of the car, drew a circle on the ground and told the blonde to stand in it and don't move. He got out a knife and cut all the new leather seats out of the car. The blonde was laughing. Then he got out a baseball bat and smashed in all the windows. The blonde was laughing even harder. He got a knife and cut all the tires. The blonde was laughing hysterically now. The truck driver said, "I just destroyed your car, why the heck are you laughing?"

The blonde replied, " Every time you weren't looking, I stepped out the circle!"

Why did the truck driver drive his truck off the cliff?
To test out the air brakes!

A truck driver tried to edge his semi past the blonde lady driver on the road ahead of him as she was obviously having difficulty deciding which lane she wanted to be in. Finally, her mind made up, the woman veered into the truck driver's lane and jammed on her brakes, which resulted in a slight collision. Unhurt but obviously harried, the blonde driver rushed over to the truck driver and started to bawl him out, barking, "You knew I was going to do something idiotic. Why didn't you stop to wait and see what it was?"

What do you get when six J. B. Hunt drivers leave a truck stop?
Twelve parking spaces.

Zek and Luke went to a trucking company to apply for a "team" truck driving job. The personnel manager decided, after talking to them both that they weren't the sharpest knives in the drawer. He decides to interview them separately. He first interviews Zek. After 15 minutes he completes the interview. Zek bearly passes. Next he interviews Luke. He begins by asking the usual transportation related questions. Luke also bearly passes. The personnel manager next interviews them both together. He presents them with this potential problem: "Now Zek and Luke, let's say that you two are a driving team. One of you is driving the rig and the other is asleep in the back. You are going down this very steep hill with sixty thousand pounds of steel on the truck. All the sudden your breaks go out and your speed is increasing. What would be the first thing you'd do?"

About a minute passes and there is no answer. Then all the sudden Luke spoke up, "I know, I know, I know the first thing I'd do."

The personnel manager says, "Yes, Luke what is the first thing you'd do?"

Luke says, "I'd wake up Zek!"

The personnel manger replies, "WHAT? Why would you wake up Zek?"

"Cause," says Luke, "He ain't never seen no big accident before!"

We heard a rumor that the J B Hunt Company was buying out Dick Simon. They're going to call it "Hunt-n-Dick"

Three drivers are killed in an accident. At the pearly gates, St. Peter asks each one; "What do you want people to say about you at your funeral?"

The first driver says, "I want folks to say that I was a good father and provider for my family."

The second driver says, "I want folks to say that I was a good teacher and that I helped my students to be good drivers."

The third driver says, "I want folks to say: 'Hey, he's moving!'"

How do truckers take a bubble bath?
They eat beans for dinner.

A fellow was following a truck in heavy traffic. Every block or so, when they were stopped at a stop light, the driver of the truck would jump out of the cab with a big stick and bang on the side of the cargo bay. He'd then jump back into the cab in time to drive away when the signal changed. The first fellow observed this for several miles, until he could stand it no longer. The next time the truck driver jumped out with the stick, the first fellow jumped out and ran up to him. "I'm sorry to bother you," he said, over the din of the banging, "but I am very curious; could you tell me what you are doing?"

Without breaking rhythm, the truck driver replied, "Sure, Mac. Ya see, this here's a six-ton truck but I've got eight tons of canaries aboard, so I've gotta keep two ton of them flying all the time so I don't break an axle."

The truck driver stopped to picked up the girl hitchhiker in short shorts. "Say, what's your name, mister?" she inquired, after she climbed up in the truck.

"It's Snow, Roy Snow," he answered, "and what's yours?"

"I'm June, June Hansen," she said. "Hey, why do you keep

sizing me up with those sidelong glances?" she challenged the trucker some miles down the road.

"Can you imagine what it might be like," he countered with a question of his own, "having eight inches of Snow in June?"

Why did eighteen truck drivers go to the movies together? The sign read: Under 17 not allowed.

A truck driver hauling a tractor-trailer load of computers stops for a beer. As he approaches the bar he sees a big sign on the door saying: "NERDS NOT ALLOWED—ENTER AT YOUR OWN RISK." He goes in and sits down. The bartender comes over to him, sniffs, and says, "You smell kind of nerdy, and asks him what he does for a living." The truck driver says he drives a truck, and the smell is just from the computers he is hauling. The bartender says OK, truck drivers are not nerds, and serves him a beer. As he is sipping his beer, a skinny guy walks in with tape around his glasses, a pocket protector with twelve kinds of pens and pencils stashed in his pocket protector, and a belt at least a foot too long. The bartender, without saying a word, pulls out a shotgun and blows the guy away. The truck driver asks him why he did that. The bartender said not to worry, "The nerds are overpopulating the Silicon Valley, and are in season now. You don't even need a license," he said.

So the truck driver finishes his beer, gets back in his truck, and heads back onto the freeway. Suddenly, as he veers to avoid an accident, the load shifts. The back door breaks open and computers spill out all over the freeway. He jumps out and sees a crowd already forming, grabbing up the computers. They are all engineers, accountants, and programmers wearing the nerdiest clothes he has ever seen. He can't let them steal his whole load. So, remembering what happened in the bar, he pulls out his gun and starts blasting away, felling several of them instantly.

A highway patrol officer comes zooming up and jumps out of the car screaming at him to stop. The truck driver says, "What's wrong? I thought nerds were in season."

"Well, sure," said the patrolman, "But you can't bait 'em."

Trucker Computer Terms:

"Hard drive" — Trying to climb a steep, muddy hill with 3 flat tires and pulling a trailer load of fertilizer.

"Keyboard" — Place to hang your truck keys.

"Window" — Place in the truck to hang your guns.

"Floppy" — When you run out of Polygrip.

"Modem" — How you got rid of your dandelions.

"ROM" — Delicious when you mix it with coca cola.

"Byte" — First word in a kiss-off phrase.

"Reboot" — What you do when the first pair gets covered with barnyard stuff.

"Network" — Activity meant to provide bait for your trot line.

"Mouse" — Fuzzy, soft thing you stuff in your beer bottle in order to get a free case.

"LAN" — To borrow as in, "Hey Delbert! LAN me yore truck."

"Cursor" — What some guys do when they are mad at their wife and/or girlfriend.

"bit" — A wager as in, "I bit you can't spit that watermelon seed across the porch longways."

"digital control" — What yore fingers do on the TV remote.

"packet" — What you do to a suitcase or Wal-Mart bag before a trip.

Chapter Seven
Truckers Slang

Ace	An important CB'er
Advertising	State Highway Patrol with lights on
Alligator	Rubber from a recapped tire
Apple	A CB addict
Aardvark	A Kenworth T-600 (AKA anteater)
Alligator	Rubber from a recapped tire
Back	Over, back to you
Back door	Rear of vehicle, last vehicle
Back down	Slow down
Back out	Stop transmitting
Back row	The area at some truck stops where hookers hang out
Bad scene	A crowded channel
Ballet dancer	An antenna that really sways
Bambi	A deer, whether dead or alive
Barbershop	A low overpass
Barefoot	CB set output signal not additionally amplified
Base station	CB set operated from a fixed location
Beam	Type of directional antenna

Bear	Policeman, State Highway Patrol
Bear bait	Leading a group of CB'ers
Bear cave	Police station or post on the highway
Bear in the air	Highway Patrol flying overhead
Bear meat	Vehicle not equipped with a CB
Bear report	Where are the police?
Bear taking pictures	Radar
Bears wall to wall	Many bears
Beast	A CB rig
Beat the bushes	Finding the "bears"
Bed Buggers	Moving Companies
Be-bop	Radio control signals
Beer tone	An intermittent tone signal
Big Daddy,	
Big Brother	Federal Communications Commission
Big Dog	Federal Marshal
Big road	A major highway
Big/Tall rubber	24 inch tires
Big road	Highway
Big truck	An eighteen wheeler
Big switch	Turn off the CB set
Big 10-4	Acknowledged with enthusiasm
Bingo cards	Paper cards that hold permits from various states
Bird dog	Radar detector
Black ice	Thick ice on the road
Bleeding	Interference from a nearby CB channel
Blessed event	A new CB rig
Blow the doors off	Pass on the highway
Bluebird	A Martin Truck company truck
Boardwalk	A bumpy road
Boast Toasties	A CB expert

Bob tail	Tractor without trailer
Bodacacious	Good signal, clear transmission
Boogie	Top gear
Bootlegger	Unlicensed CB'er
Boss man	Immediate supervisor
Boulevard	Interstate highway
Boy scouts	State Police
Break	I'd like to break in, interrupt
Brake check	A sudden slow down in traffic
Breaker broke	May I use this channel
Break fetish	Rides with a foot on the break
Break one-oh, break 10	I want to talk (on channel 10)
Breaker	CB'er who asks to use a channel
BTO	Big Time Operator
Bug out	To leave a channel
Bulldog	A Mack Truck
Bushels	One-half; 20 ton load would be 40 bushels
Buttermilk	Any kind of beer
Bumper sticker	A car following to closely
Bundled out	Loaded very full
Cabbage	A long steep incline in eastern Oregon
Camera	Radar unit
Can	Shell of a CB set
Cartel	A group hogging a channel
Cash register	Toll booth
Catch	Talk to
Cell block	Location of base station
Chain gang	Members of a CB club
Channel 25	Telephone
Charlie	The FCC

Cheese wagon	School bus
Chicken coop	Truck weigh station
Chicken lights	Extra lights on the truck and trailer
Chopped top	Short antenna
Chrome dome	Mobile unit with roof antenna
City kitty	Local police officer
Clean	No Highway Patrol around
Clean cut	Unmodified rig
Clear Out	Final transmission
Coffee break	Unoranized CB social gathering
Come again	Return call, repeat
Comeback	Return call
Comedian	The median strip
Come on	Over, you may transmit
Comic books	Truck driver's log book
Commercial	Prostitute
Container	Chassis and shell of CB rig
Corn flakes	Consolidated Freightways truck
Cotton picker	Used instead of four letter words on air
County Mounty	County sheriff or highway patrol
Covered up	Interfered with
Covered wagon	A trailer with a tarp cover
Cowboy	Driver constantly changing lanes at high speed
Cradle baby	CB'er afraid to ask for standby
Crotch rocket	A motorcycle
Cub scouts	Sheriff's men
Curly locks	Coils on a CB rig
Customer	Vehicle stopped by police
Cut out	To leave a channel
Cut the hoax	Turn off CB set
Daddy-O	The FCC

Darktime	Night
Deadhead	Miles that you won't get paid for
Desperado	Someone being arrested
Destruction zone	Construction zone
Diesel car	Eighteen wheeler
Despair box	Box where spare CB components are kept
Dirty town	New York City
Do it to it	Accelerate a vehicle
Don't tense	Take it easy
Double Harley	Channel 11
Do what?	I did not copy your last transmission
Down stroke	A hill going down
Dragon fly	A truck with no power. Drags uphill, flys downhill
Dragon wagon	Tow Truck
Driver	Refers to the person you are talking to
Drop deck	Open trailer with two levels
Dry box	A freight trailer or van
Ears	CB set
Ears on	CB radio turned on
Eat-um-up	Truck stop cafe
Eighteen wheeler	Diesel truck, all semi-trailer trucks
Eights, eighty-eights	Goodbye, love and kisses
Eighty fifth street	Highway I 95
ERS	Emergency Radio Service
Eyeball	Face to face meeting
Evil Kenevil	Police on a motorcycle
Fat load	Overload, more weight than local state law allows
Feed the bears	Get a ticket
Final	Last transmission

Fingers	A channel hopping CB'er
Fire in the wire	An Amplified AM transmission
Five-five	Speed limit, 55 mile per hour
Flappers	Ears
Flat bed	Straight open trailer
Flip flop	A U-turn
FM	FM/AM radio
Fog lifter	Interesting CB'er
Four	Abbreviation of 10-4
Four-ten	10-4, emphatically
Four wheeler	Passenger car
Fox Charlie Charlie	The FCC
Freightshaker	A Freightliner truck
Friendly Candy Co.	FCC
Front door	Leading rig in a convoy
Fugitive	CB'er operating on a different channel
Full grown	DOT officer
Garbage	Produce
Gearjammer, Gearslammer	A speeding truck driver
General mess of crap	GMC trucks by Volvo/White
Geological survey	CB'er looking under his seat
Georgia overdrive	Neutral gear
Getting out	Being heard
Going horizontal	Going to bed
Glory card	Class D license
Go juice	Diesel fuel
Gone	Final transmission or switching to another channel
Good buddy	Homosexual
Good neighbor	Person you are talking to
Goon squad	Channel hoggers

Go to the Harley	Go to channel 1
Gouge on it	Go fast, step on it
GP	Ground Plain antenna type
Grab bag	Illegal hamming on CB
Granny lane	The right lane or slow lane on the highway
Grass	Median strip or side of the road
Green stamp road	Toll road
Green stamps	Dollars, money paid in fines
Greasy side up	A car or truck flipped over
Ground pressure	Weight
Gumball machine	Lights on a police car
Hag feast	Group of female CB'ers on channel
Hammer	Accelerator
Hammer down	Driving fast
Hammer lane	The fast lane or passing lane on the highway
Hamster	One who "hams" on CB
Hand	Driver
Handle	Slang names used by CB'ers
Happy happy	Happy New Year
Happy number	An S-meter reading
Harvey Wallbanger	Reckless driver
Haulin' dispatcher brains	Pulling an empty trailer
Having shutter problems	Getting sleepy
Hit the jackpot	When police lights are flashing
Henchmen	Group of CB'ers
High gear	Use of amplified power transmitter
Ho Chi Minh Trail	California highway 152
Holler	Call
Home twenty	At home
Honeys	Attractive females

Honey bear	Female police officer
Hood	Any conventional tractor, as opposed to a cab-over
Hound men	Police looking for CB'ers using rigs while mobile
How about	Calling
How am I hitting you?	Are you receiving my transmission?
Hundred dollar lane	The left lane of a highway with more than two lanes in each direction
Hung up	CB'er who can't leave set
Idiot box	Television set
In the big hole	In top gear
In the grass	Parked or pulled over on a median strip
Invitations	Traffic tickets
Jamboree	Gathering of CB'ers sponcored by a CB club
Junk yard	Scrap metal hauler
Juvenile Delinquent	Someone pretending to be a trucker
Keep it between the ditches	Drive safely
Keep Smokey out of your britches	Look out for speed traps
Kenosha Cadillac	Any car made by AMC
Kenworthless	A Kenworth truck, also; K Wopper
Keyboard	Controls of a CB set
Key down	When you try to talk over someone who is transmitting
Keyed	Pressing the microphone button
Kojak with a Kodak	A police officer with a radar gun
Knuckle Dragger	Driving too slow
Land line	Telephone
Lay a land mine	Bathroom break/Take a shit

Large car	A big fancy truck
Lay an eye on	See
Left coast	West coast
Let the channel roll	Let others break in and use the channel
Linear	Extra power amplifier used to increase
CB output	
Local Smokey	
Local Yokel	City police officer
Lot lizard	A truck stop hooker
Lumper	Someone who unloads trucks
Mail	Overheard conversation (reading the mail)
Make the trip?	Is my transmission being received?
Mardi Gras	Welfare check day
Meat wagon	Ambulance
Mercy, Mercy sakes	An exclamation
Merry merry	Merry Christmas
Mile markers	Small signs that indicate the distance along the highway
Mission	A rush load
Mix-master	Highway cloverleaf
Mobile	In motion
Modulate	To talk with
Monitor	Emergency assistance, channel 9
Moth ball	Annual CB convention
Motion Lotion	Fuel
Move	In motion
Mud duck	Very weak radio signal
Negative, negatory	No
Negative contact	Station being called fail to respond
Negative copy	Did not hear your last transmission
Ninety fifth street	Interstate 95

OM	Old man CB'er
On the move	Driving, moving
On the side	Parked or pulled over on the shoulder
One-eyed monster	Television set
One time	For a short contact
Other half	Husband or wife
Over shoulder	Behind
Panic in the streets	Area being monitored by the FCC
Parking lot	A truck carrying automobiles
Party row	Area at some truck stops where hookers hang out
Pass the numbers to you	Best wishes to you
Peanut butter in your ears	Not listening, can't hear
Penman	CB applicant who has filled out FCC forms
Peter pleaser	Homosexual
Peter pleasin' pickle park	Rest area where homosexuals hang out
Pickle Park	Rest Area
Pickum-up	Light truck, pickup truck
Picture machine	Radar
Picture taker	Radar
Plain wrapper	Police car with no markings
Play dead	Stand by
Politz-eye	The police
Pounds	Number on S-meter indicating output, S-3 is three pounds, ect.
Power up	Thank you very much
Pregnant roller skate	Volkswagen
Prescription	FCC rules

Pull the big one	Signing off for good
Pumpkin	Schneider company trucks
Put the good numbers on you	Threes and eight's: best regards
Putting on	Strength of signal
Put the pedal to the metal	Accelerate
Q-bird	An intermittent tone generator
Radio check	Reception
Rake the leaves	Back door or last vehicle in a string
Rascal	Someone you know
Ratchet jaw	Non-stop talker
REACT	A national group of volunteers who monitor channel 9
Read	Hear
Readin' the mail	Just listening to the CB
Recessional reptiles	prostitutes or hookers
Reefer	A refrigerated cargo trailer
Rest-um-up	Roadside rest area
Rig	CB radio, also tractor
Riot squad	Neighbors with television interference
Road pizza	A badly mangled road kill
Rocking chair	Vehicle between two CB vehicles
Roger	I acknowledge
Roger ramjet	A speeding car
Roger roller skate	Passenger car going more that 20 miles per hour over the speed limit
Roller skate	Small car
Rolling parking lot	automotive transport
Rooster cruiser	A male driver, looking for another man for sex

Salt shaker	A snowplow that spreads salt and dirt on the road
Sand baggin'	Listen in on a channel without talking
Sand box	A gravel trailer
Savages	CB'er who hogs the channel
Scatterstick	Vertical antenna with ground plain
Scoot	A Harley-Davidson motorcycle
Schneider eggs	Orange drums used in construction areas
Seat covers	Occupants of a passenger car, usually attractive females
Semi automatic super 10	Type of transmission in which some of the gears change automatically
Sesame Street	CB channel 19
Set of dials	CB rig
Seventy three	Best regards
Shake the leaves	See what's ahead
Shakey Town- Shakey Side	Los Angeles, California
Shanty shaker	Mobile home mover. Also known as a mobile modular residential commercial transportation relocation technical specialist
She bear	Female police officer
Shim	To illegally soup up a transmitter
Shinny hiney	Trailer with polished metal doors
Shoot you in the back	When a hidden cop uses a radar gun after you pass
Short-short	Soon
Shout	Call
Side piece	A linear amplifier

Sidewalk weenie washer	Homosexual
Six wheeler	Mid-sized truck or van
Skateboard	A flatbed trailer
Ski, short trip	Conditions permitting long distance contacts
Skins	Tires
Slaughter house	Channel 11
Slave drivers	Cb'ers that take control of a channel
Slider	An illegal VFO (variable frequency oscillator)
Slip seating	Changing drivers without stopping the truck
Slow wheels in the fast lane	Swift Company drivers
Small rubber	22 inch tires
Smokin' scooter	A motorcycle cop
Smokey	Smokey the Bear", police
Smokey on four legs	Mounted police
Smokey with ears	Police listening in on a CB
Snooperscope	An illegally high antenna
Sonnet	CB'er who advertises products on the air
Souped up	A radio modified to run illegally high power
Stagecoach	A tour bus
Stack them eight's	Best regards
Stand on it	Accelerate very quickly
Stepped on you	Another CB'er transmitted at the same time
Struggle	Trying to "break" a channel
Sucker	A CB rig on the service bench

Sunbeam	A CB'er who livens the channel with witticisms
Super trooper	Officer pulling more than one car over at a time
Sure enough store bought large car	A big fancy eighteen wheeler
Swamp donkey	A moose
Sweeping leaves	Bringing up the rear
Swinging	Carrying a load of carcass beef
SWR	Standing Wave Radio
Taking pictures	Radar
Tearjerker	A CB'er who always cries the blues
T-bone	Side impact crash
Tennessee Valley Indians	TVI - Television interference
Ten roger	I acknowledge
Thermos bottle	Tanker truck
Thin	A very weak signal
Thin man	A CB'er with a weak carrier
Thirty three	10-33, this is an emergency
Trash wagon	Garbage truck
Thread	Wires in a CB rig
Threes on you	Best regards
Threes and eight's	Heavy regards
Throwing	Transmitting
Ticker tape	FCC rules
Ticks	The minutes (each tick is 60 seconds)
Tijuana taxi	Well marked police car
Tin can	CB rig
Tooled up	A souped up rig
Too many eggs in one basket	Overweight

Toothpicks	Lumber
Train station	Traffic court that fines everybody
Travel agent	Dispatcher
Trip	Strong signal
Trucker Buddies	National association of drivers, trucking companies and schools working to education children about the trucking industry
Triple digit truck	A truck that can exceed 100 miles per hour
Turkey day	Thanksgivings day
Turkey call	Intermittent tone generator
Twenty	Location
Twin pots	A CB'er who has two sets from the same manufacturer
Two-way radar	Radar used from a moving police car
Two wheeler	Motorbike, motorcycle
Ungowa Bwana	Okay
VW	A Volvo/White truck
Walked all over	Overpowered by a stronger signal
Wall to wall	Peg full scale on S-meter, loud and clear
Wally World	A Wal-Mart truck, store or distribution center
Warden	Wife, husband, or FCC
We gone	Stopping our sending, will listen
Wheels	The mobile unit
Weirdy	A homemade CB rig
West Coast turnarounds	Benzedrine pills or speed
Wiggle wagons	Double or triple trailers
Willy Weaver	A drunk driver
Windjammer	A long-winded CB'er

Window wash	A rainstorm
Wrapped loaf	A CB rig in its original carton
Wrapper	Paint job on a car
XYL	Ex-young lady; wife
Yard	Company parking lot
Yard dog	A driver who moves trailers on a company's lot
Yardstick	Mile markers
YL	Young lady
You got a copy on me?	Do you hear me?
Youngville	Young children using this channel
Zoo	Highway patrol headquarters

Chapter Eight
Trucker Cities and National 10 Codes

The Big A	Atlanta, Georgia
Air Capitol	Wichita, Kansas
Armadillo	Texas
The Alamo	San Antonio, Texas
The Astrodome	Houston, Texas
The Apple	New York New York
Bean Town	Boston, Maryland
Big D	Dallas/Fort Worth, Texas
Big O	Omaha, Nebraska
The Bikini general	Miami, Florida or Florida in
Bright Lights	Kansas City, Missouri
Bull City	Durham, North Carolina
CB Town	Council Bluffs, Iowa
Cigar City	Minneapolis/St Paul, Minnesota
Cowtown	Calgery, Alberta, Canada
(The) Flag	Flagstaff, Arizona
The Friendly	Philadelphia, Pennsylvania
(The) Gateway	St. Louis, Missouri
Gold City	Goldsboro, North Carolina
Green Bay	San Francisco, California

Guitar	Nashville, Tennessee
Hog Town	Toronto, Ontario, Canada
Hotlanta	Atlanta, Ga
Irish	South Bend, Indiana
Little Richard	Macon, Georgia
Mardi Gras	New Orleans, Louisiana
Mile High	Denver, Colorado
Motor City	Detroit, Michigan
Music City	Nashville, Tennessee
Capital City	Raleigh, North Carolina
The Big Smoke	Hamilton, Ontario, Canada
The Dirty	Cleveland, Ohio
The Mistake on the Lake	Erie, Pennsylvania
The Nickel	Buffalo, New York
The peg	Winnipeg, Ontario, Canada
Philly	Philadelphia, Pennsylvania
The Rubber	Akron, Ohio
Shaky City	Los Angeles, California
Smoke City	Birmingham, Alabama
Steel City/Town	Pittsburgh, Pennsylvania
The Swamp	Montreal, Quebec, Canada
Windy	Chicago, Illinois

National 10 codes

10-0	Caution
10-1	Unable to copy
10-2	Signals good
10-3	Stop transmitting
10-4	Acknowledgment; okay
10-5	Relay message
10-6	Busy, stand by
10-7	Out of services
10-8	In service, on air
10-9	Repeat message
10-10	Fight or disorder reported
10-11	Dog case
10-12	Stand by
10-13	Weather and road report
10-14	Prowler report
10-15	Burglary
10-16	Domestic problem
10-17	Meet with complainant
10-18	Quickly
10-19	Return to...
10-20	Give location
10-21	Call on telephone
10-22	Disregard
10-23	Arrived at scene
10-24	Assignment completed

10-25	Report in person (meet)
10-26	Detaining subject, expedite
10-27	Drivers license info
10-28	Vehicle registration info
10-29	Check stolen/wanted
10-30	Unnecessary use of radio
10-31	Crime in progress
10-32	Subject with firearms
10-33	Emergency
10-34	Riot
10-35	Major crime alert
10-36	Correct time
10-37	Investigate suspicious
10-38	Stopping suspicious
10-39	Urgent, use lights and siren
10-40	Silent run, no lights or siren
10-41	Beginning tour of duty
10-42	Ending tour of duty
10-43	Information
10-44	Permission to leave
10-45	Animal carcass
10-46	Assist motorist
10-47	Emergency road repair needed
10-48	Traffic standard repair
10-49	Traffic light out
10-50	Accident
10-51	Wrecker needed
10-52	Ambulance needed
10-53	Road blocked
10-54	Livestock/ carcass on road
10-55	Intoxicated driver
10-56	Intoxicated pedestrian

10-57	Hit and run accident
10-58	Direct traffic
10-59	Convoy or escort
10-60	Squad in vicinity
10-61	Personnel in area
10-62	Reply to message
10-63	Prepare to make a written copy
10-64	Message for local delivery
10-65	Awaiting you next message/ assignment
10-66	Message cancellation
10-67	All units comply
10-68	Dispatch information
10-69	Message received
10-70	Fire alarm
10-71	Advise nature of fire
10-72	Report progress on fire
10-73	Smoke report
10-74	Negative
10-75	In contact with...
10-76	Enroute
10-77	ETA (Estimated Time of Arrival)
10-78	Need assistance
10-79	Notify coroner
10-80	Chase in progress
10-81	Breathalyzer request
10-82	Reserve a room for...
10-83	Working school crossing
10-84	If meeting_____, advise ETA
10-85	Delayed due to...
10-86	Officer/operator on duty
10-87	Pick up/distribute checks
10-88	Telephone number

10-89	Bomb threat
10-90	Bank alarm
10-91	Pick up prisoner/subject
10-92	Improperly parked vehicle
10-93	Blockade
10-94	Drag racing
10-95	Delayed due to....
10-96	Mental subject
10-97	Check signal
10-98	Prison/jail break
10-99	Wanted/ stolen indicated
10-100	Five minute break; bathroom
10-101	Medical acknowledgment
10-102	Send rescue units to...
10-103	Send police units to...
10-104	Unable to locate
10-105	Patient refuses service
10-106	Patient refuses treatment
10-107	Patient pickup by other means
10-108	Transfer patient from__ to___
10-109	Patient condition codes
10-109A	Walking but injured
10-109B	Moderate injury
10-109C	Severe injuries
10-109D	Dead
10-110	Multi-injury accident
10-200	Police needed at...